VIEWS · FROM · A · FRENCH · FARMHOUSE

·Views · From · A · French · Farmhouse ·

Photographed by Carey More · Written by Julian More

PAVILION

FOR SHEILA AND CAMILLA

First published in Great Britain
in 1985 by Pavilion Books Limited
196 Shaftesbury Avenue, London WC2H 8JL

This edition first published in 1986

Photographs © 1985 Carey More
Text © 1985 Julian More

Translations by Julian More

Designed by Bernard Higton

Map art work by David Williams

A CIP Catalogue record for this book is
available from the British Library

ISBN 0-907516-63-7 (H/B)
ISBN 1-85145-031-9 (P/B)

Printed and bound by Kyodo, Singapore
2 4 6 8 10 9 7 5 3

CONTENTS

Introduction 6
Carey More, Julian More

SPRING
'…March is the month above all; for then France,
who never stops working, begins her spring cleaning,
loppings and prunings…'

RUDYARD KIPLING *Souvenirs of France*

SUMMER
'…they drank the bottle of wine while a faint
wind rocked the pine needles…'

F. SCOTT FITZGERALD *Tender Is The Night*

AUTUMN
'Let us cry Long Live The Sun·which gives us
such a beautiful light.'

CEZANNE *A letter to Emile Zola*

WINTER
'…a bah-ing outside tells us Midnight Mass
has just finished and that the shepherds are bringing
their lambs back, blessed beneath their capes.'

COLETTE *Belles Saisons I*

THE DAYS ARE ROUND

Acknowledgements 142

I N T R O D U C T I O N

There is something magical about the luminosity and space of Provence, a slowness of tempo ordered by nature not man. Because of my love of nature and the land, it is in the country that I feel my soul.

Getting up when it's still dark to catch the dawn light is exhilarating; to be a solitary figure in a vast landscape feeling the wildness, the force of nature. There is not a sound, all is silently alive. I try to capture this with my camera. I must feel it or the image will have no life.

Some days I see nothing I want to photograph, no photographic compositions present themselves. Chance is not with me, nature cannot be forced.

Other days, I've felt almost privileged, as if I was being shown image after image. Perhaps a foggy dawn gives way to mist which touches everything with radiance as the sun burns through. Or a shepherd and his flock appear in a landscape. Or clouds cast patterns on the land. Moments like this are worth hours of waiting.

I was photographed by Norman Parkinson when I was only six months old. Of course I do not remember this, but ever since I can remember I've been interested in photography. I modelled for several years, travelling all over the world, and was lucky enough to work with some of the most respected photographers. Picking up photographic techniques during this period, I also began to develop my own style of photography.

I still travel a great deal, and my camera is always with me. As Cartier-Bresson says, photography is a way of life.

My first photographs of Provence were taken in December 1981. Later I thought about making them into a book, and over the next three years, I returned many times to capture the different seasons.

From the hogsback behind our house, the landscape rolls back like a magic carpet – west to the Cévennes, north to the Drôme, east to Mont Ventoux, south to the Dentelles. Two hundred kilometres on our doorstep. We have grandstand views of lightning, sunsets, rainbows, full moons, storm clouds.

My folio of pictures grew, and with it the idea of collaborating with my father. We both wanted to express our love for this part of the world, he with his writing, I with my photographs. We joined forces.

CAREY MORE, Visan 1984

FONTVIEILLE, AUTHOR AND PHOTOGRAPHER AT DAUDET'S MILL

I have collaborated with some strange people in my time. Never a daughter until now. It is very exacting. Some views were on our doorstep, others a walk up the hill, but the furthest no more than two hours' drive. I was the driver. Often the days began in darkness.

> 4.00 a.m. Visan.
> Alarm clock shattering my sleep. Stagger to bathroom. Forestalled by Carey, already brushing teeth. Camera equipment litters landing. We're off on another shoot, our first objective an hour's drive – dawn on Mont Ventoux. Start out through swirling mists. House more like Wuthering Heights than southern France at this early hour.

The Brontës would have been quite at home in our eccentric climate. But it was a local writer whose work suggested the theme of our book – Jean Giono. Our days were long in working hours; but I prefer Giono's phrase 'the days are round' which evokes something more fulfilling – not a mere labour but a labour of love.

For a photographer, Provence can throw up as many weather hazards as Yorkshire. Hailstones big as golfballs once nearly shattered my windshield, as I travelled south on the autoroute near Montélimar where Mediterranean weather officially begins. A stormy entry into Provence presages its unpredictability: swift changes from white, hot light to glowering clouds; from soughing breeze fragrant with pine and herb to temper-fraying, lip-chapping mistral; as with the southern temperament, violence beneath the gaiety, luckily more often expressed in manic revving of motorcycles than murder.

Elements and people are unpredictable, yet there is an inevitability that circumscribes the surprises: the round-ness of the days; changing light at each hour; the rotation of crops – olive, wheat, lavender, peach, tomato, melon, grape. A sense of Season prevails.

> 5.30 a.m. Mt-Ventoux.
> Carey sets up shot, all a mystery to me. Dawn eerie and moody. The great mountain in misty silhouette, ghostly, living up to its occult reputation, hobgoblins invisible but present.

Typically unpredictable was the purchase of our farm-house. For several years, my wife Sheila and I had been searching southern France. What we could afford, we didn't like; what we liked, we couldn't afford. One day, I was writing in the gardens of the Hotel Beffroi, Vaison-la-Romaine, when Sheila spoke the ritual words 'I think I'll go and find us a house.' Anywhere south of Montéli-mar one of us always said it. House-hunting had become a sort of addiction. It was a habit neither of us could kick.

The house, the agent told us, was surrounded by vines and had bizarre décor. The garden was a wasteland; the

well yielded only three buckets of water a day – one for the animals, one for the cooking, one for the washing; and the kitchen beams were painted orange and blue. We were not put off; it took less than five minutes to know this was finally it; that mysterious, atavistic recognition of home occurred.

> 9.00 a.m. Sault.
> Bright sunshine. Carey shoots man reading newspaper, woman with *baguettes* of bread. To lavender field. This is Giono country, high and harsh in winter, dazzling purple now. In shade of cherry tree read Giono's *'Rondeur des Jours'*.

Our farmhouse is on the vine slopes of Visan, a Côtes-du-Rhône village whose wine has been chosen by the Sunday Times Wine Club. Visan is proud of its wines' increasing success abroad but the pride of the region, Vaucluse, tends to insularity. Anyone, like us, who hails from more than twenty-five kilometres away is not just a stranger but a Martian.

Among the early Martians were papal dignitaries from Avignon. A small peninsular of Vaucluse juts north into the Drôme, known as the Enclave of the Popes. Our eccentric geography happened thus: in 1317 the French Dauphin sold Valréas, our nearest town, to Pope John as a nice, cool summer home for his sweating cardinals in Avignon. Visan was part of the package. The furious French King Charles, the Dauphin's father, put an instant stop to his son's property dealing. And, to this day, a desirable residence can be hard for a Martian to find in the Enclave.

Martians or not, its only British residents have had nothing but kindness from Visan. People were quick with offers of tractors, trucks, and strong arms. I was soon known as *le Julian* by our nearest winegrowing neighbours, Pierre and Yves. Sheila, who has made a garden grow from a wilderness, swops cuttings with Pierre's wife. The family come to Sunday lunch which must, on their insistence, be one hundred percent British – roast lamb and mint sauce, followed by apple crumble.

Neighbours are neighbours; Yves, seeing a strange car here during our absence, sharply interrogated its owner who turned out to be our builder, who at once sharply interrogated Yves; a noisy, night-time marauder in the garden was confronted by Pierre with shotgun – and turned out to be a hungry badger.

> 12.00 p.m. Simiane-la-Rotonde.
> Sun too high for colour. Carey changes to black and white. I'm getting hungry, but she is unflagging. Graveyard blossoms with plastic flowers. Sit on grave beneath shady cedars. I shall join its tenant if I don't eat soon.

Long after loved ones are supposed to have quarrelled,

broken up, and gone their separate ways, here we were once again setting up a family home. Although Carey and her sister Camilla had spent most of their lives in cities, there was something about Visan which made us all instantly respond to the call of the Provençal country-side.

High Provence, Provence of the plains and the sea coast and the rivers – that vast area once occupied by the Romans, their 'Provincia'; the Midi, all-embracing word for the warm south, the cold south, the south in all its myriad manifestations; Vaucluse, the department in which we live. Terms I had always used loosely now had concrete meaning, a look, a sound, a smell. And, in the variety of our terrain, it struck me what a variety of writing there was about it too.

It seemed I would enrich the book by sharing it with other writers who have southern France in their blood. I began reading and re-reading my favourites, not so that Carey's photographs should illustrate them nor they comment on her images, but so that we should free-wheel through the seasons in the leisurely manner that Provence or the Midi or Vaucluse demands.

Like a hunter surveying his hunting-grounds, I stood on the hogsback behind our house: to the west Robert Louis Stevenson country; to the east Jean Giono country; to the south Alphonse Daudet country; and so on. I began to make my literary map.

1.30 p.m. Revest-Les-Brousses.

Too hot for work. Collapse beneath Martini parasol of Auberge du Marcassin. It means 'young wild boar'. Carey wants light lunch. We get young wild boar. The sacred ceremony of the midday blow-out.

In the roundness of these days we moved through the changing light, taking in the luminosity which, for centuries, has drawn artists and writers here like a magnet. It illumines the essential quality which makes Provence special. The Romans called it 'Genius Loci', spirit of place: Lawrence Durrell has used it as a title; we celebrate it in poetry and pastis.

7.30 p.m. Visan.

Return from shoot exhausted. Find Sheila spraying cypresses against the mystery disease which is killing off so many conifers. Neighbour Pierre up from his farm with sulphur for our young vines. A couple of pastis with Pierre, then plan tomorrow's shoot.

Tomorrow, yesterday, today, seasons, years all have their roundness. There is a constant motion in us, as in our trees. Nothing stands still, it never means quite the same. Carey and I try to encapsulate the moment, this feeling we have for our home. With camera, with words. And, above all, with love.   JULIAN MORE, Visan 1984

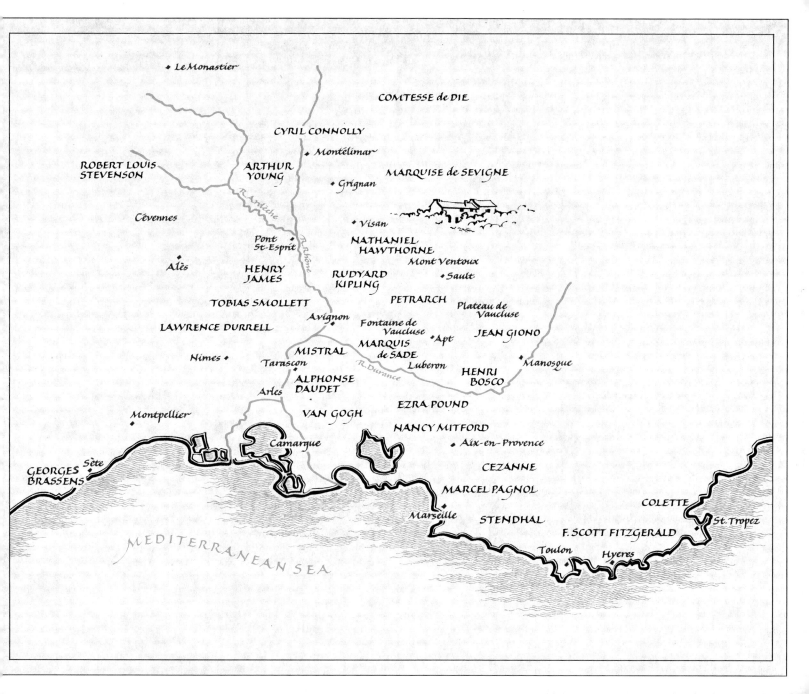

MOLLANS-SUR-OUVEZE

Days begin and end in the dead of night.
They are not shaped long, in the manner of things which lead to
ends – arrow, road, man's life on earth. They are shaped
round, in the manner of things eternal and stable – sun, world, God.
Civilization tries to persuade us we are going towards
something, a distant goal. We have forgotten that our only goal is to
live, to live each and every day, and that if we live each and
every day, our true goal is achieved. All civilized people see the day
beginning at dawn or a little after or a long time after or
whatever time their work begins; this they lengthen according to
their work, during what they call 'all day long'; and end it
when they close their eyes. It is they who say the days are long.
On the contrary, the days are round.

JEAN GIONO, *'Rondeur des Jours'* (1943)

· S P R I N G ·

Days have their roundness, so do years. And for me, the Provençal year runs its cyclic course from spring to spring. It is an entirely pagan theory of mine; the gods are as firmly in the earth here as God is in the churches. Belief in both is double security against a May frost. Our New Year's Day has no fixed date; it depends on the occurrence of that first golden dawn of silence, that glorious no-man's-day between winter and spring. We are eager for it. We uncreak.

We wait for it expectantly after promising signs: in mid-February the first asparagus at Carpentras market; in late February the first fragile almond blossom coming with light snowfalls; occasional lunches on the terrace in brilliant sunshine, but wrapped up as if we were at St-Moritz.

The southern French winter is by no means what it was cracked up to be by the British in my great-aunt Bessie's day. She was a gambler at Menton, a white-clad,

CAIRANNE

black-spectacled remittance lady clocking into the Casino punctually and clocking out equally punctually, a few francs up or down on the day. Her family, I remember, were envious of her apparently sun-blessed winters: as she spent the entire day, each and every day, at the roulette wheel, she never saw the howling, storm-tossed Mediterranean outside, and consequently reported all her days as halcyon.

So much for climatic myth. The first golden dawn of spring is a reality. Winter's grip mysteriously loosens. Winds drop. Hurtling red rooftiles no longer threaten our skulls. Wafts of woodsmoke down gusty village alleys give way to encouraging smells of fresh-baked bread. A burgeoning baker's wife talks suddenly of births and lottery wins instead of arthritis and funerals.

Wild marigolds, grape hyacinths, minute wild irises less than two inches high are in the fields. Rosemary blooms everywhere, attracting clouds of bees. And writer's cramp relaxes in the spring sunshine.

'In April all the trees were in blossom. I was enchanted. Beneath a cherry tree I could see a ladder. A woman had climbed it, plunging head and hands in among the youngest leaves,' wrote Henri Bosco, Provençal novelist of Italian origin, describing spring as the high season of love.

'Now and again, for no good reason, a great handful of petals would make their random departure. Floating from a cluster of flowers, they fell to the ground and scattered. The warm breeze awakened flowers, perfumes, insects, and went on to stir up the nests. There thousands of birds sang, throats open to the young wind, on that hill of gardens.' (*Le Jardin d'Hyacinthe*).

On such a day writers blow dust off their typewriters – if they can find time to write: Colette in love, newly

CHERRY TREE

arrived at La Treille Muscate, her St-Tropez retreat, greets the shock of the Provençal spring with the excitement of a child. 'I knew nothing of the serene season's invasion and conquest, that lasting treaty between warmth, colour, and smell.' (*Bella-Vista*)

On such a day I imagine that Anglo-Irish romantic, Cyril Connolly, in his *salade niçoise* days, 'peeling off the kilometres to the tune of "Blue Skies", sizzling down the long black liquid reaches of Nationale Sept, the plane trees going sha-sha-sha through the open window, the wind-screen yellowing with crushed midges, she with the Michelin beside me, a handkerchief binding her hair...' (*The Unquiet Grave*)

And surely on such a day Alphonse Daudet bought his windmill at Fontvieille. Native of Nîmes, Daudet hated the mid-nineteenth century grime and literary mud-slinging of Paris, and a renewed love for his birthplace is expressed in *Lettres de mon Moulin*.

Some of these short pieces earthily convey spring awakenings, both tender and tragic. *Les Etoiles* may seem somewhat winsome to our jaded tastes, but I am reminded of my own first love and that terrible gawky yearning: the poor, horny, young shepherd has to spend a night on a mountain with his master's daughter, whom he secretly loves but cannot have. 'All around us, the stars

ALPHONSE DAUDET'S MILL

went on their soundless way, as orderly as a great flock on the move; and now and again, I imagined that one of those stars, the brightest, had strayed from the path and come to rest on my shoulder to sleep...'

Daudet was master of the short story. And in *L'Arlésienne*, a tragedy in five crisp pages, the wild girl from Arles drives a country boy to suicide. Victorian mores have not much changed: southern machismo expects brides to be virgins, and the male takes the best seat in the room; yet society is matriarchal, women on a pedestal. Contradictory and perverse, this attitude to women is

SIMIANE-LA-ROTONDE

understood by Daudet. 'Jan never spoke again of the girl from Arles. But he still loved her; and more deeply than ever since knowing she had once been another man's mistress.' Off her pedestal, the girl has an added erotic distinction.

To this day the girls from Arles have a wild look, darker and more Mediterranean, with the long, straight noses of their Greek antecedents. And the boys have Roman names – Marius, Sylvius, Octavius. In spring, the bars are jumping in Carpentras, Michael Jackson booming in Bollène, motorcycles thrust-and-buzz along the stony tracks of Vacqueyras vineyards with unhelmeted girls a-pillion, black curls flying in the wind; courtship is noisy and vital in Provence. It is the sound of sap rising.

Curiously the Provençals have a reputation for reserve: it is not much in evidence in spring. Though God help anyone who tries a casual pick-up; he may find a whole clan, thumbs in their jeans belts, waiting for him in his hotel room before he can even get the girl there. The reserve is southern and practical: what heats fast may boil over. And passion is kept under control, to be consummated later.

There is a Provençal saying: 'Girls conceive in August, married women in January.'

Spring courtship rituals are more literary than anthro-pological. How romantic really was romantic love? What did the Provençal troubadours get up to with those bored ladies of noble birth, languishing while their husbands were off on a Crusade? Merely serenade them with medieval pop songs? Hardly.

That extraordinary woman in a man's world, the one and only lady troubadour, the Comtesse de Die, is quite explicit when she sighs:

'I would love to hold my Knight
One night in my arms all bare.
He would rest from his delight ·
On a cushion of bosom fair.'

Confessionals were hot in the twelfth and thirteenth centuries, and a fallen lady loftily named Ysolt or Rixende would afterwards hie herself to a nunnery called the Nobles Dames at Aix, there to do luxurious penance with pearl-studded rosary and golden missal. Leaving her troubadour, like a medieval Bob Dylan, to protest in song: 'God confound thee, Rome! Thou forgivest sins for money!'

Another enigma – closer still to the Church: what exactly was the relationship between Petrarch and his beloved Laura? An Italian poet-priest attached to the Pope's Court in Avignon, Petrarch made a habit of having

AIGUEBELLE, TRAPPIST MONASTERY

his cake and eating it. On the one hand, he condemned the louche prosperity Avignon had found as host to the Popes, proliferating with bawdy-houses and sexual intrigue. ('God is despised; they worship money...everything breathes lies: the air, the land, and above all the bedchambers.') Yet at his country retreat, Fontaine-de-Vaucluse, the priest fell hopelessly in love with a fourteen-year-old girl called Laura and instead of keeping it quiet flaunted his illicit amour in a ceaseless flow of sonnets.

Petrarch already had two illegitimate children from the kind of wild living in Avignon he claimed to despise. He met Laura on a country walk on Good Friday. He was twenty-three. She was a teenager with cheeks of 'roses plucked by virgin hands'. Their courtship lasted twenty-one years until her death, after which he was inconsolable.

A mystery surrounds the relationship, which we are led to believe was unconsummated. Did the pious Laura refuse him because he was a priest? Or perhaps it was this very reason that attracted her, and there was a delicious complicity of frustration between them, good for his writing, if not her happiness.

Apart from the sonnets, Petrarch stunningly evoked his love of the countryside. Of his farm, he wrote: 'It isn't big, but it's honest.' He relished the silence of the fields and the perpetual murmur of the river, and climbing Mont Ventoux on a May day in 1336: '...at first vividly struck by the unfamiliarity of the air I breathed and by the vastness of the panorama, I shifted my gaze: clouds floated at my feet. From there, I turned my eyes towards Italy, the direction of a longing heart. Spiked and snowy Alps appeared quite close to me, despite the great distance.'

MONT VENTOUX

ROUSSET-LES-VIGNES, DESERTED FARM

And all over this vast area of Provence, much of it visible from the top of Ventoux, the language of love was Provençal, encouragingly known as the langue d'oc – 'the language of yes'.

It is a mellifluous derivation of Latin – a spoken, slangy, popular version for whores, peasants, and poets. Curiously its sound is closer to English than French, and its diphthongs and double-syllable rhymes make it easier to translate into English.

Mar que reboumbello	Waves of roaring ocean
Bos plen de rumour,	Whispering woods above,
Digas à la bello	Tell my heart's emotion
Moun langui d'amour.	To my lady love.

With France's increasingly heavy hand in Provençal affairs of state, the Provençal language diminished in popularity for five centuries. Racine, passing through Valence in 1661, was relieved to see a sign 'French Spoken Here'.

In the nineteenth century it staged a brief, heady revival. This was largely the work of Frédéric Mistral, the epic poet of Maillane, and his group of cultural devolutionists who called themselves Félibres. The Félibres were passionately anti-Paris and pro-all-things-Provençal like Pistou soup, hearty dancing of a *farandole* and the non-killing bullfights (*ferrada*) of the Camargue. They were bold, brash, and naïve.

It was the divine right of poets, according to Mistral, to whoop it up all over the countryside, carousing at Châteauneuf-du-Pape or song-singing in the ruins of Les Baux. 'Poets wrote the psalms!' he would declare proudly to any church-cat killjoy. And when the rumbustious mood flaked, Mistral's mother, who spoke only Provençal, cooked Pistou for them at the modest village house of this dashing peasant member of that Olympian literary body, the French Academy.

To make sense of Mistral, you need to have fluent Provençal. I don't. So I am not equipped to comment on the poetry. To twentieth century writers like Jean Giono, Mistral appears academic, his Provençal revival giving an untrue, folksy image of Provence.

Giono was born at Manosque before the First World War when peasant society still prospered. His father, an artisan of Italian origin, gave him an intensive course in the sensuality of nature – flora, fauna, and human – and a solid grounding in the Classics.

But Giono's writing is never nostalgic; he hates that hankering for the mythic good old days. Equally he

PISTOU SOUP

PLATEAU DE VAUCLUSE

'Spring sprang suddenly onto the land. Green daffodils appeared above the grass. Wild rose bushes trembled beneath large blooms. The air was bitter and sharp as the fig-tree's sap.' *(Que Ma Joie Demeure)*

When Giono writes about sap rising, it is sensual, atavistic. Man and earth are one: 'He is firmly implanted in the land – like a column' are the last words of *Regain*. Its peasant hero has finally mastered his land; the earth is feminine, the man at one with her, in her.

If nowadays we have lost touch with the animal world, Giono had not. He equated much of its behaviour with ours. A horse feeling the desire to mate 'will look at the sun and the sun will brighten his eyes. He will sniff the wind of May and the wind of May will stay wafting through the recesses of his bones and head. Thus will he go to the edge of the field. He will be totally surrounded by freedom.'

Also in *Que Ma Joie Demeure*, a doe waits for her first mating, which occurs during a hunt, the duality of life and death ever present. 'The little doe on heat, motionless in the shadows, began to cry as at the approach of a

would hate the commercial greed of modern Provence, the smog-rotting Aix, the shimmering mirages of chemical plants round the Etang de Berre. Giono is his own man, an original, his Provence a tableau of invention neither past nor present, timeless, anarchic, deeply physical. Conmen, craftsmen, clowns, aristos, murderers, peasants, prostitutes, dreamers live round their days and years and lives with inevitability.

PLATEAU DE VAUCLUSE, JEAN GIONO COUNTRY

LE PONT D'ARC

long sleep. The hunting-horn sounded. On the other side of her tears, beneath the moon, the world shimmered like mountains of water. A black shape sprang at her. She recognized something living and male.'

Giono turns spring into a hunting season. The prey can be animal or human. But the hunter must know how to attract it. 'He had a special springtime voice which came from his throat; she was made for that call.' And then he goes after her.

'There is the path, the track of a woman. She is there on that tiny thread of land between the grass. He lets out a laugh which makes no noise, his hunter's laugh. He laughs because he knows how to read these things written in the air and on the earth.' *(Regain)*

The classic image of woman-hunting has served writers well from Homer onwards. And in *Jean Le Bleu* Giono transposes the Helen of Troy legend to the village of Corbières. Its baker's wife is swept away by a handsome Italian to an island in the Durance river. Instead of judging her behaviour, the villagers persuade her to come back, as the baker can no longer bake without her. 'Love is all very well,' says their spokesman, 'but we've got to eat.'

I first encountered this tribute to French common-sense in its movie version *La Femme du Boulanger* at my school cinema club when I was fourteen. I fell in love with Aurélie, the baker's wife, played with that irresistible combination of lust and innocence by Ginette Leclerc. I also date my love affair with Provence from this screening.

Its director-scenarist, Marcel Pagnol, has been accused by Giono purists of debasing a Homeric epic into a weepy star vehicle for the great Provençal actor, Raimu, who played the cuckold baker. Orson Welles called it the most beautiful film he had ever seen. Anyway, Pagnol's friendship with Giono survived the typical showbiz

FAUCON, OLIVE TREES

ding-dong between film director and novelist, and Pagnol went on to make *Regain* in 1937.

Marcel Pagnol, schoolmaster's son, timed and placed his birth well for a cinéaste – Marseille, 1895 – on the very day Louis Lumière was showing the first ever moving picture.

His Marseille trilogy *Marius, Fanny,* and *César* began by causing a theatrical stir on the Paris boulevards, because for the first time Midi people were not being portrayed as lovable buffoons but real flesh-and-blood with their own sharp wit and fiery emotions. These

VISAN

movies won international success, rare in the French cinema, and *Fanny* was even turned into a Broadway musical, about as evocative of Marseille as clam chowder.

Set almost entirely in a waterfront bar, Pagnol's was a love saga of directness and bitter-sweet humour, with Chekovian attention to domestic detail. The ingredients of a fish soup, the right glass for pastis, a well-baked loaf of bread, take on as much importance as a mistress's infidelity, a son's betrayal, or a believer's doubts about God.

Fanny: Love's not everything. Some things are stronger than that…

Marius: Yes, money.

Fanny: Money, the sea…

Marius: We all go towards the things we love. You're marrying Panisse's money and me, I'm free, I'm marrying the sea. Yes, that's best for both of us…

Meanwhile life goes on. César is serving an order in his bar:

César: And a bottle of local white wine.

M. Brun: If it's chilled.

THE CAMARGUE

César: If it's chilled? Feel that! You'd think it came from the vineyards of the North Pole.

While César gives the impression of nesting in his bar, his son Marius lives up to his Roman general's name – with his eagerness to be off to sea and conquer foreign parts, satisfying his restlessness before his love for Fanny.

Sap rising also has its disturbing side, the movement of nature stirs, and – like the transhumance of the animals, the return to green pastures from winter quarters – we feel the urge to be up and doing. To be photographing, writing, sowing the Morning Glories and Belles de Nuit,

derusting and painting the garden chairs, putting the bamboo covering over the terrace to protect our heads from the sun. The sun comes nearer, light is sharper. It is like a great, inexorable opening-out.

'I immediately feel the effects of this strange exhaltation of natural powers,' wrote Henri Bosco, who rivals Giono in his evocation of the spirit of place. Bosco speaks mystically of the spring's movement in the secret body of the world and the influence of planetary forces. 'I have to take refuge at the back of the old farmhouse which, in its old age, is less susceptible to the earth's drunkenness.' (*Le Jardin d'Hyacinthe*)

Bosco imbues his Provençal spring with a disturbing new energy. In *Le Mas Théotime* the tension becomes almost unbearable. A boy watches the playful chase of his childhood sweetheart by other boys; he cannot see exactly what is going on, can only hear sounds:

'I would have liked to fly to her rescue, for a consuming jealousy tortured me; but my pride was stronger than my concern and I waited. Soon the cries stopped and a long silence reigned. Then Geneviève left the orchard, pale, her hair tousled, and came forwards, staggering. And I burst into tears.'

Bosco's question: how can we hope to bring our will to bear on the forces of nature if we have no control over our

IMPROMPTU STREET THEATRE

BANON, FORTIFIED TOWN

SEGURET, COURTYARD WITH PLANE TREE

own nature? The solid old farmhouse is a winter haven from the elements but nothing can protect us from spring awakening and its emotional havoc.

Equally restless, Vincent Van Gogh in letters from Arles to his brother, Theo, is inspired by the air of April to a fever of painting, a driven man aware of his need for self-improvement, yet unconscious of his own genius:

'I have a fresh orchard…apricot trees of a very pale rose.' Rose-coloured trees, but never seen through rose-coloured spectacles. 'I must reach the point where my pictures will cover what I spend, and even more than that, taking into account so much spent in the past. Well,

it will come. I don't make a success of everything, but I'm getting on.'

Also with an uneasy edge, American poet Ezra Pound's troubadour poetry has violence in it. 'Damn it all! All this our South stinks peace!' protests Bertran de Borns in *Sestina: Altaforte*. He finds music in the clashing of swords and is eager to be off to war, not 'rot in womanish peace'. In medieval times you made love *and* war; if the machismo offends, the restlessness we can sympathise with.

'And I love to see the sun rising blood-crimson.
And I watch his spears through the dark clash
And it fills my heart with rejoicing
And pries wide my mouth with fast music
When I see him so scorn and defy peace,
His lone might 'gainst all darkness opposing.'
(*Sestina: Altaforte*)

Provence had its own prince of darkness – the Marquis de Sade, a notorious eighteenth century visitor to the area between prison sentences for perverse sex. In spring he was rumoured to be on the rampage from his château at Lacoste. Local girls – boys, too – steered clear of him. 'They have spread it abroad in Avignon,' wrote the testy Marquis, 'that from morning to evening I've been routing

St-Roman-de-Malegarde

LACOSTE, MARQUIS DE SADE'S CHATEAU

all the neighbouring towns, terrifying everyone. I'm considered a werewolf here.'

Was de Sade victim of a witch-hunt? He thought so. And it was the witch who did the hunting – his mother-in-law: her influence at Court resulted in lengthy prison sentences out of proportion to his crimes. No wonder he sided with the Revolution.

The château at Lacoste, now part-ruin, part-contemporary music college, stands on the sinister north slope of the Lubéron, that long high hogsback between Mont Ventoux and Montagne-Ste-Victoire. Here de Sade lived with his wife. The Marquise de Sade, suffering her husband's infidelities in silence, must rate as the original masochist. Whatever his cruelty in love – and many claim it was exaggerated – he was certainly an astringent letter writer. 'I had a pretty girl to dinner,' he wrote to a friend, 'but as you didn't turn up, you don't deserve to know her name.'

From the Marquis de Sade to milder animals: the great spring transhumance is in progress.

'M. Seguin had never had luck with his goats. He lost them all in the same way; one fine morning, they broke their ropes, went to the mountain, and up there the wolf ate them.' (Daudet: *Lettres de Mon Moulin*)

Not all goats are as foolhardy as M. Seguin's. But all goats are full of the joys of spring. 'She placed her four feet in front of the cypress; she threatened it with a movement of her horns, then dashed off in the opposite direction and the grass whistled against her legs.' (Giono: *Regain*)

I have seen in the Drôme goats leading the sheep on a difficult path. It was like a tribe on the move: the shepherd had a donkey, carrying his clothes, his food, and the new-born lambs not yet strong enough to walk so far. The bells tinkled into the distance, as the flock went on and up to higher grazing, and then there was no sound but the gentle wind.

COMPS, GOATS RETURNING TO THE HILLS

· S U M M E R ·

Summer is the season of the stranger. Foreigner and stranger are the same word in French – *étranger*. Strangers from Spain to help with the harvests, strangers from Italy to sing in the festivals, strangers from Algeria to visit other strangers from Algeria, strangers from Holland, Belgium and Britain to plod about the Roman remains.

The Romans' Provincia gave Provence its name, superimposed imperial pomposity and lumpen bourgeois civilization on a land in search of identity, and did very little to help her find it. The monuments perpetuate the Roman presence as a far vaster legacy than that of any other stranger.

I cannot look at the overwhelming triumphal arches, celebrating victories over the barbarian hordes without picturing the Roman General Marius, on the advice of his prophetess, hurling his prisoners off Montagne-Ste-Victoire as a human sacrifice; even Cézanne cannot disguise something sombre about that mountain with its haunted precipice. Bread and

Montagne-Ste-Victoire, Cezanne Country

VALAURIE

circuses, blood and cries. Not all the peristyles or aqueducts or columns can make me admire Emperor Augustus; the amphitheatres at Orange and Vaison-la-Romaine only come to life at festival time when Barbara Hendricks' voice soars into the moonlight, or Dizzy Gillespie's trumpet strikes a most unmilitaristic note.

Cultural heresy, perhaps. I share it with André Breton who went even further and refused to set foot in Italy because of the five-century Roman occupation. Quite a sacrifice.

Giono wrote: '…it's not necessary to know the date the church got its porch, or of that triumphal arch with the frothy billowing of a deep-rooted wheatfield beneath it. There is no history. Nothing need be explained. Time passes only in the movement of a watch.' There is more joy in one lavender field in July, with the mist rising – its perfume, the sound of bees, the cool of morning – than in ten triumphal arches.

So we are suspicious of the harm strangers can do, being strangers ourselves bringing our own strange customs – aerobics on the lawn, two veg. with the meat, hot baths more than once a week. Beware the stranger. Bosco finds him a threat, too. He comes, he goes, like the mistral, making us edgy and uncertain. He is not necessarily evil, just different, which is worse. The sky is bluer when he leaves. Even if he has taken your possessions.

Petrarch describes a fourteenth century burglary: 'Pious bandits that they were, wishing by the spoils of their theft to make a sacrifice to Laverna, goddess of thieves, even on Christmas day they pounced on my ill-guarded country house and took everything they could carry, burning the rest.'

Vaucluse, six centuries later, is second only to the Paris region for burglaries in France. Our house has sixteen stout shutters; they are closed paranoiacally every night. Against the stranger.

SAULT, LAVENDER FIELD

Shortly before his premature death, I saw George Brassens, twentieth century troubadour of the music hall, at my Paris local, the Bobino. Native of Sète on the Languedoc Coast, Brassens was like an affectionate anarcho professor, ageless and popular, grey-moustached and pipe-smoking. His tunes, to a relaxed guitar and bass, were warm and lyrical, his words were poetic. Like Giono, he was most at home beneath a tree in Provence. Here he is, at his most astringent, singing *The Ballad of People Born Somewhere*.

It's true that it's charming, that small village square,
All those burghs, those hamlets, those towns and their
    sights.
They've only one fault, that's to have people there,
In their castle and church, on their beaches and heights.
And to have people there who do not want to know
The others they pass with their heads in the air,
That chauvinist race, with its colours on show,
Those poor happy fools had to be born somewhere.

Americans, like Ezra Pound, escaped the puritan stuffiness of the New World to find a freer creative and moral spirit in the Old. Scott Fitzgerald spent a year in southern France, and told the 1924 readers of the Saturday Evening Post *How to live on practically nothing a year.*

It cost him a fortune, but what a year! 'When you first set eyes on the Mediterranean,' he wrote, 'you know at once why it was here man first stood erect and stretched out his hands towards the sun.'

Scott was not always so purple.

' "Hasn't it been a good summer!" said the young man lazily. "We've become absolutely French". "And the French are such aesthetic people," said the young lady, listening for a moment to the banana music. "They know how to live. Think of all the nice things they have

VALAURIE, FOUNTAIN AND WASH-HOUSE

SIMIANE-LA-ROTONDE

TULETTE, MARKET DAY

to eat!" "Delicious things! Heavenly things!" exclaimed the young man, spreading some American devilled ham on some biscuits marked Springfield, Illinois.'

In a narrative as psychologically complex as *Tender Is The Night*, there is not much room for spirit of place. Yet suddenly we fall upon a poetic fling of brilliance: Nicole Diver 'feeling good from the rosy wine at lunch' in a summer garden takes 'a walk marked by an intangible mist of bloom'; 'they drank the bottle of wine while a faint wind rocked the pine needles and the sensual heat of early afternoon made blinding freckles on the checkered luncheon cloth'; 'The others helped him carry the lamps up – who would not be pleased at carrying lamps, helpfully through the darkness?'

It never ceases to amaze me that a terrain of such wide open spaces – plateau, marshland, garrigue, mountain, plain, river, lagoon – can inspire such intimate writing. The stranger seems really to belong, to feel at home in simple yet important rituals. Picasso and Miró referred to Provence as their *quartier*, as did Bosco – an artist's quarter, like Montparnasse or Montmartre where people were close-knit in the common cause of art, no matter where they originated.

Cézanne, the native of Aix, and Van Gogh, the

stranger from Holland, were both after the same re-valuation of fundamentals, both working at roughly the same time in the same *quartier*. The landscape of Aix is very different from that of Arles; Cézanne concentrated on the world he saw, the earth of his forbears, in him, around him; Van Gogh had wider, more cosmic vision. Yet the subject and inspiration of both painters is unmistakably their *quartier*.

Van Gogh, writing to Theo in August 1888 has a feeling of being in his own skin – 'and in my hide within the cog-wheels of the Fine Arts, like corn between the millstones.' His Provence is '…to feel the stars and the infinite high and clear above you. Then life is after all almost enchanted. Oh! those who don't believe in the sun here are real infidels.'

By June the following year, Van Gogh had been committed as a mental patient at Saint-Rémy, where he continued to work. 'This morning I saw the country from my window a long time before sunrise, with nothing but the morning star, which looked very big.' He always wanted to make a journey to the stars, which on a moonless summer night seems possible, so close are they. 'If we can take a train to Tarascon or Rouen, we take death to reach a star.' That does not read like the letter of a suicide, rather of a strong human spirit whose adaptabil-ity to his surroundings would make him no more a stranger to Heaven than Provence.

Aspects of the British, odd as it may seem, are exotic to the French – le kilt, Burberrys, le five o'clock, Buckingham Palace (its sex-life, especially), La Dame de Fer (not hers), le porridge, and Lawrence Durrell.

Provence's best known celebrator in English lives near Nîmes. He is the archetypal expatriate writer. His poems celebrate Lesbos, Alexandria, Corfu, Rio, Sarajevo, Avignon. His *Elegy on the Closing of the French Brothels* is naturally dedicated to Henry Miller, and he belongs, like Anthony Burgess, to that red-blooded school of English writing where bawdy and brains are inseparable.

Durrell is too romanesque for gothic literary tastes. Not everyone can take his Mediterranean exuberance. It is as vivid as the Provençal fabrics, derived from Indian prints which traders brought here long ago. Born in India, Durrell takes from his careers as diplomat, scholar and nightclub pianist with an eclecticism of which Anglo-Saxons are deeply suspicious, fearing it may lead to excess. Which it does.

Going too far is Durrell's ace. Like Giono, he has invented his own Provence, no less sensual. 'The first time we made love was among the rhododendrons at the Pont du Gard.' (*Livia*) Durrell breathes life into a

SABLET

Roman monument, and I forget the coachloads of Japanese in jeans and dark glasses swarming among those self-same rhododendrons trying to squeeze each other and the Pont into camera frame.

'When she was pregnant with their second child, they ran away to France and played at being artists in a secluded *mas* near Avignon – two months of bliss. She let herself go, was dishevelled and out of breath as she bent over the cooking pots, while he reverently prepared the vegetables. Her breasts were full of milk from which he drew frequent swigs.' (*Livia*)

Durrell's Provence is peopled with exotic Anglo-French upper class, as at home in raunchy, backstreet Avignon as in a decaying château in the Alpilles.

But he can also touch us way below *la vie du château*. In search of a herbal cure for eczema, he describes Monsieur Ludovic Chardenon, (*the plant-magic man*) of Arles: 'I saw him as belonging to that obstinate tribe of men, the

GRIGNAN, MARQUISE DE SEVIGNE

creative yea-saying ones, who are obstinately holding the pass in Provence and elsewhere until the rest of us come to our senses and decide what we want to live for, and with, and how.'

It is a heartfelt, simple plea for the quality of life. And here, because it is so potentially good, we feel all the angrier with the spoliators, that pall of smog over the Rhône valley, the stench of autoroute back-ups.

Not that we ourselves make any pious claims to travel by pony-cart and generate our own electricity by water-wheel. But now it is high summer. And in high summer we live a sort of château life of unreality. The Provençal dream? Some might not think so from reading the Marquise de Sévigné.

That entertaining and bitchy letter writer first descended on her daughter, Madame de Grignan, at their wind-swept château on the plain below us in the summer of 1672. She did the bone-shaking, hair-raising coach-and-barge journey from Paris in a record seven-

HILLS OF THE DROME

GRIGNAN CHATEAU

teen days; the high speed train now takes under three hours. Leaving the lush life of Paris salons, the Marquise writes, 'I've gone down to Provence to see Grignan; greater love hath no woman.'

But she found compensations there, mostly in bossing her daughter about from sunrise to sunset, a long time in midsummer. Madame de Grignan was married to the Acting-Governor of Provence, whose thankless task it was to get the Provençals to pay their taxes to the French King, and he had enough problems without a literary mother-in-law.

The Marquise thought her daughter should love no one but her. She nagged her incessantly about her health, marriage, child-births, and even tried to persuade her to leave the Midi. She described losing her daughter as a theft. 'God give me grace some day to love Him as much as I love you.'

But Madame de Grignan, knowing her place was with Monsieur, soldiered on, and eventually her mother accepted even the discomfort and draughtiness of the François Premier suite. For Madame de Sévigné, Grignan came to seem like a paradise compared to the rest of rural France, a bogland of squalor at the time. 'One sees neither misery nor famine nor poor. One imagines oneself in another world.'

GRIGNAN, GARDEN HUT WITH WATER PUMP

And she also grew quite fond of the house, on which the unfortunate Monsieur de Grignan, encouraged by mother-in-law, spent so much money in improvements that he went broke.

After the Second World War a fictional château in Provence gives a hero's welcome to its returning Seigneur, with his English wife, child and nanny. Nanny, in Nancy Mitford's *The Blessing* takes an instant dislike to the villagers: 'Funny looking lot, aren't they? Not too fond of washing, if you ask me. Fearful smell of drains, dear.' It gets even worse, when Nanny is installed in the nursery. 'Aren't the stairs awful? I shan't be able to manage them many times a day in this heat. Well, I've been trying to unpack, but there's nowhere to put anything, you know – shame, really – no nice shelves for our toys. No mantlepieces, either, for my photographs and the ornaments. Funny sort of rooms, aren't they? Not very homey. I'd like to show you the bathroom and lavatory, dear – nothing but a cupboard – no window at all, really most insanitary – it would never be allowed at home.'

The potty-trained grow less fastidious in the sun and the pleasures of doing as the Romans didn't (they were like Nanny about their plumbing), peeing in a vineyard by moonlight, bathing in a gorge pool, are the small pleasures of more modest homemakers, like ourselves and Colette.

As arbitrarily as I make the beginning of our year occur in spring, so do I stretch the east of our territory to St-Tropez – in order to include Colette. The coast lost its pleasure for me one gorgeous summer's day, out in a boat, everything perfect, until we decided to drop anchor in a secluded bay; up and down went the anchor as we tried to find water unpolluted by melon rind, plastic sacks of garbage, and oil slicks. When Colette wrote of it in the twenties, St-Tropez was still a fishing village.

JONQUIERES, YOUNG BOULES PLAYERS

MONT VENTOUX, WHITE PEBBLE SUMMIT

ARLES RESTAURANT

Colette had a special instinct for the soil and its creatures; she also knew exactly what a Provençal home should have. 'In Provence they protect themselves against too much light, narrow the passage of sun and insect life…and there is a merciful negligence which gives it an impromptu charm in which the temporary and the permanent collaborate, plant life and grey stone patched with dusty pink plaster.' (*Belles Saisons I*)

At La Treille Muscate, her house near St-Tropez, Colette reckoned that peasant houses in need of repair fixed themselves up, but only with peasants living in them; we strangers go through the agony of plaster chippings, endless dust and mud and spending more than we reckoned. Prices tend to go up faster than the houses can get fixed up.

Be thankful for the garden. 'Two hectares of vine, orange, green fig, black fig,' Colette found on her doorstep. 'Having said that garlic, peppers and aubergines

abound in the furrows between the vines, will I have said all? There is also a house – small, one storey – but that's less important than that the terrace is covered with wistaria, for example, or that flame-red bignonia and mimosa bushes with big trunks, running from the gate to the front door, honour it with their presence.' (*Prisons et Paradis*)

Thoughts of a summer garden are never far from fears of a summer drought – and the water problems. Water, in the Midi, is the currency of friendship. Without it, you need friends. With it, you make friends. Our own well dried up one August. Guests from the north arrived to stay. 'Not *any* water?' they exclaimed, extra white. 'Only from the village fountain,' we said. Luckily they were old friends, and the twice daily jerrycan run added a chin-up-and-carry-on zest to their holiday, like the Desert Rats with their half glass of water a day.

Eventually a proper water supply had to be piped from

VISAN, BRIDGE HOUSE

THE CAMARGUE

drons, their beds seething with what life remained – squirming salamanders, spiders, water-flies all fighting for a wet corner.' (*Lettres de Mon Moulin*).

Midi water, with its importance in the fight for survival, has had its own mythology since pagan times. There is much strange folklore about the water of Mont Ventoux, for instance. Friends of ours have a spring of holy water nearby; their house was named after it, Les Saintes Fonts. The water is said to be specially curative for the eyes; even in Roman times pilgrims came to have their blindness cured. Indeed our friends' pool is quite unlike any other; the body feels unusually relaxed after a swim in it, the eyes clearer.

'In the water of the clear fountain, she bathed in the buff…' sang Georges Brassens; and Jean Giono finds even a water shortage has its compensations. 'He began soaping his face. The foam was violet. Jaume looked at him. "What are you shaving with?" "Wine, what else?"'. And for quenching a thirst – 'We only drank wine; and the parched gullets constantly wanted more. And the thirst persisted.' But there is nothing quite like the joy of falling upon water. 'With arms outstretched he embraced the overflowing basin, stuck his mouth to a crack in the stone surround; between gulps he whimpered with pleasure like a child at its mother's breast.' (*Colline*)

150 metres below ground; there was no guarantee of striking it either, no diviner, just blind faith and a geologist's survey to encourage painless payment as we drilled deeper and deeper.

It paid off, in more ways than water. In exchange for letting our drainage disappear beneath his vines, our neighbour Pierre gets a supplementary water supply from us; the pipeline is like a blood-link between us, an artery of friendship.

Alphonse Daudet describes the Camargue in August, marshes dried up, white mud cracked and creviced. 'All over, the ponds sizzled beneath the sun like huge caul-

ETANG DE GALABERT, BIRDS OF THE CAMARGUE

Feuds over water are commonplace. Here is a Giono peasant, in *Rondeur des Jours* discussing a feud with friends. '"They've been at it two years. There's only one spring in all the fields of Auvailles. Whose is it? Who knows? It had to end in this." They heard the shot of a rifle, then a noise of broken glass.'

In autumn and spring, water can strike terror as swollen rivers, Ardèche and Durance, hurtle towards the Rhône their flotsam of cattle carcasses and uprooted trees. In summer, the terror is not just water shortage, but forest fire. Who has not been moved by images of charred and desolate coastline, all because some idiot stranger cooked a barbecue in a tinder-box pine forest?

Between May and September we can be arrested for lighting a bonfire of so much as one leaf. It is a wise law. The firemen are all volunteers: Jean, a black-moustachioed bear of a man with a soggy brown butt of Gauloise permanently in the corner of his mouth, can be called out any time of the day or night, not just for forest fires, but also for road accidents, suicides, or to get rid of our hornet's nest. They do not like careless strangers. Or careless locals, for that matter.

'It started like God's thunder, over there, between two villages burning their potato haulm…like a supple beast it sprang across the heath … all day and part of the following night it broke the boys' arms and exhausted their minds. As the day dawned, they saw it, more vigorous and happy than ever, twisting through the hills its huge body like a tidal wave; it was too late.' (*Colline*)

Classical duality is nowhere more in evidence than in Provence, and even today there is an unspoken respect for the mysteries of the elements. Water drowns and quenches; earth nourishes and buries; fire burns and cooks.

And with its fire, that same summer sun, for which we strangers came here, blisters our bodies and ripens our fruit. 'You breathe not air, but leaves, fruit with the bitter-sweetness of scented berries, bark, fruit-tree's pith. You breathe whole hedgerows; you breathe fresh sap of plum, pure juice of peach, milk of almond and essence of pear.' (Bosco: *Sylvius*)

For Bosco and Giono, harvest time is both hard and joyous. Giono calls corn and olive oil the gold of the poor; in *Regain* a primitive hunter becomes a man by cultivating his corn. But it is no gift from the gods. A long passage in *Rondeur des Jours* describes the hard grind as a whole village – youngest to oldest, even the ancient priest – sweats for its corn. Up at three in the morning, under a sun that gruels by nine, on through the hallucinating day till aching limbs crash out for the short night's sleep.

FOAL IN CAMARGUE GRASS

VESC

ST-TRINIT

Day after day, in the rhythm of the scythes moving through the corn, it loses its colour – 'The corn is grey. The sun strikes full-force. Fists tighten; feet advance. Hands collect the corn. Arms make the sheaf. A hand takes the binding, fingers tie the knot, a shoulder tosses the sheaf, a hand takes the sheaf by the binding, an arm pulls it, a shoulder lifts it, a hand puts it on the pile of sheaves.'

It is this evocation of sheer hard agricultural labour which makes Giono the literary soul-mate of Thomas Hardy. Today, of course, combine harvesters do the job described above. But I recommend anyone at a comfortable office desk, dreaming of that deserted farm on the Vaucluse Plateau, reclaimed as a paradise of organic aubergines and free-range ducks, to read Jean Giono before handing in his notice.

A surprising August visitor was, in fact, a farmer – an English farmer at that. Arthur Young, son of a Suffolk squire, was an eighteenth century radical agronomist and critic of French landowners' abuses, who after the Revolution became adviser to the Jacobin government on agricultural matters. Can anyone imagine, in the present prickly context of the Common Market, a Brit advising President Mitterrand on how to bring down the cost of milk-fed baby lamb?

It was quite an adventure. 'They could not conceive',

REILHANETTE, YOUNG GOATHERD

wrote Young in 1789, 'why a Suffolk farmer should travel into the Vivarais. Never had they heard of any person travelling for agriculture. They would take my passport to the Hotel de Ville; have the permanent council assembled; and place a sentinel at my door.'

Young ploughed on, but grizzled about the service and the weather with characteristic Britishness. Despite 'the proverbial politeness of the French', he found trouble in restaurants: 'not one time in forty will a foreigner, as such, receive the slightest mark of attention.' And as for the mistral – 'at four or five in the morning, it is so cold that no traveller ventures out. It is more penetratingly drying than I had any conception of.'

So don't believe all you read in the Guide Michelin: the mistral *does* blow in August. It also rains on the wine festivals, hails on the fireworks, and thunders on the bullfights. It is sad for the sodden campers and sopping opera-singers and other outdoor strangers. In this hectic and unreliable month, I try to practise the art of doing nothing. It is very difficult. I should learn from that sybaritic lover of Provence, Cyril Connolly – 'Others merely live: I vegetate.' (*The Unquiet Grave*)

Monteux, Festival Fireworks

·AUTUMN·

Suddenly peace reigns. The strangers have gone. And it is time to welcome the second spring, that phenomenon of nature which, in the year that I write, brings roses rampaging for the second time on our sun-baked, shabby pink pebbledash. Colette loved this moment, and even if tired waiters yawn and not all the débris of summer is yet black-sacked, prices do come down and flowers do come up. 'September's spring sees the reflowering of climbing nasturtiums, roses, the tireless multicoloured purslane and little rambling petunias.' (*Belles Saisons I*)

No longer does Apt market on Saturday morning play host to Le Tout Lubéron, modishly homespun in dress but otherwise behaving as if they were at Paris's latest in-spot.

Come September, in the rustic-chic second homes of Gordes and Oppède-le-Vieux that Vivaldi score is taken from the harpsichord; the early oil by Bernard Buffet is returned to the bank; bottles are removed from the mill-wheel cleverly converted into a pool bar; and the BMW is packed with genius children, the olives Maman

APT, RUSTIC-CHIC VISITOR

bottled, and the pastis Papa brewed. For another year the simple life is over.

And now that the super-chic of the Lubéron, the campers and festival freaks have gone, a veil of silence settles over the land. If it is true that the stars make music, then this is the time to try and hear it.

Henri Bosco is not so relieved by these departures as I am. 'Little by little I had observed the new nature of silence. A person who has gone, even a quiet person, leaves a lack in the everyday sounds of a house. A footfall or a sigh you can no longer hear creates an absence, a regret.' (*Le Jardin d'Hyacinthe*) Country sounds meld naturally with the silence. 'The

silence had reached over the whole Trières area. A woodchopper was working up there in the forest. He made no more noise than a bird tapping its beak on the bark of a tree.' (Giono: *Rondeur des Jours*)

The haze of summer lifts and we begin to see our big distances again; the world seems to be at peace in the stillness. Autumn, in recent years, has regaled us with one calm, sunny day after another. Giono, had he been alive today, would have been an avid supporter of the European Peace Movements, closely allied as they are to conservation and the quality of life. In *Le Deserteur*, his deserter is not just quitting the army but bourgeois society for a purer life, an artist giving pleasure to peasants by doing paintings for their churches. At the end of *Le Grand Troupeau*, the soldiers sing joyfully 'Fuck war, long live life and anarchy.'

In 1939 Giono was arrested as a conscientious objector and imprisoned in Marseille, passing what he reckoned were 'some of the most beautiful hours of my life'. After the war he was accused of being both a dangerous Red *and* a collaborator with the Nazis. He was neither.

Autumnal Provence, in the stillness of these photographic images, reminds us how fought-over this land has been, surviving bandits, persecution, imperialism,

VISAN, VILLAGE AND PLAIN

'At about five, my wretched arthritis wakes me: to the side of me, the cypress sleeps, outlined against a pale green dawn. It neither shivers, nor breathes in its obelisk's repose. It will wake late, encouraged by the beginning of the mistral, and I shall be soothed by it.' (*Paysages et Portraits*)

Autumn does, of course, have its lesser bangs – namely, the hunting season. The trigger-happiness of the French hunter is a joke even to the French; Swiss soldiers sleep with rifles by their bed, French hunters sleep with a shotgun by theirs. It is why country property is so well defended.

Any still Sunday in September the air is rent with fusillades against the unfortunate thrush, who has the bad luck to make a most delicious paté.

In the eighteenth century this excessive slaughter was just as bad. '...one would think that every rusty gun in Provence is at work, killing all sorts of birds,' complained Arthur Young, 'the shot has fallen five or six times in my chaise and about my ears.' Stendhal, in *Mémoires d'un Touriste*, mocked the so-called hunting-lodge of the Marseille bourgeois: 'He builds a hide of hawthorn and twigs, twenty feet from his dead tree; he crouches there from four o'clock in the morning and waits patiently for a

and revolution. I often have a feeling of being on hallowed ground, land where peace and independence have been bought at a high price. Nearby Nyons has the finest olives in France. And the olive is Athena's tree, the tree of wisdom – and peace.

Now, over a distant ridge, when the haze has cleared, we witness the unwelcome return of the puffing white smoke from Pierrelatte Nuclear Power Station, reminding us how tenuous our peace is. Colette's mornings were threatened by no big bangs, rather were they made soothing by the sigh of the cypress:

ROUSSET-LES-VIGNES, RUINED FARMHOUSE

thrush to land on the dead tree. Sometimes, between four o'clock in the morning and midday, he has the pleasure of killing maybe three thrushes.'

Two centuries ago it was the same complaint: where has all the game gone? Recently our Indian summers have killed the scent, with their dryness, and such weather apparently first occurred around 1946, just when everyone was starting to talk of changed climates owing to the Atom Bomb. 'That year, the summer seemed to have passed into autumn in its entirety. Never in the memory of man had such fine weather been seen.' (Bosco: *Le Jardin d'Hyacinthe*) Only the hunters hate it.

Or is the absence of game owing to over-hunting? Perhaps there is not the respect for female game there was in Giono's day. When Panturle in *Regain* sees pregnant does running for cover, 'he let them in peace because he was a hunter and that was his livestock they were carrying there in their bellies.' Whatever the reason – pesticides, pollution, over-hunting, it is certainly the act of man, not the animals.

COUSTELLET, TOWARDS THE LUBERON

VISAN, BONFIRE

St-Martin-d'Ardeche, the Ardeche River

BONNIEUX

Since the arrival of the Aix-Nice autoroute, the hills between it and the sea have been almost depopulated of wild boar, because the natural migration from High Provence now has this barrier; a sensible wild boar knows a French driver is as unlikely to stop for him crossing the road as for a pregnant female – of any species.

I was therefore astonished to encounter a wild boar in the Massif des Maures. At five o'clock in the darkness of an autumn morning, driving along a forest track between damp-smelling chestnut trees on my way to a truffle hunt, I was suddenly confronted by an immense hulk in the headlights. The wild boar forced me to a sharp standstill, because I would have doubtless come off worse in a collision; nostrils flaring, he breathed a huge breath of surprise, steamy in the humid morning air, and lumbered sleepily off. He had not liked being woken. He was probably very old, last survivor of a dying line, having migrated long before the autoroute had exiled him from his own kind.

Bosco describes a huge mythic wild boar, 'head weighing 140 pounds, bristles like barbed wire and the shoulders of a bison'. It is the beast of late autumn, violent and threatening, analogous to the months of storm, the cathartic explosion and release from the great heat. The topographical shape of the Lubéron even resembles a wild boar, and is romantically said to exhale the smell of the beast from the damp brambles and juniper bushes on its sides.

Due ceremony is accorded to a mythic beast's dispatch, and Giono describes the final ritual of a wild boar hunt: 'They skinned it while still hot and shared the meat in handfuls. And the men washed their hands in the trough of clear water.' (*Colline*)

Partridges, according to Marcel Pagnol in *La Gloire de Mon Père*, are the prey of priests. Man of the world as well as of God, the village priest displays unexpected expertise: 'My father was a great hunter, so that's why I know. This partridge is not the *Caccabis Rufa* which is much

St-Ambroix, Poplar Trees

smaller. It's the *Caccabis Saxatalis*, that's to say the rock partridge, also known as the Greek partridge, and in Provence, the *Bartavelle*'. Later Pagnol's Uncle Jules cracks a false tooth on shot still in the *Bartavelle*, now roasted, and can only be consoled by the astonishing news – Pagnol's family being anti-clerical – that the village priest is a partridge buff.

The Marquise de Sévigné, visiting Grignan in the September of 1694, had her fill of good game, too. 'These partridges are fed on thyme, marjoram, and every scent one finds in one's sachet; no matter which. I say as much for our plump quails, whose thigh should come away from the body at the first summons (they never fail one) and our turtledoves, quite perfect too.'

The British are inclined to pooh-pooh French hunting, perhaps because less associated with horsiness than their own blood sports. The French eat horses, after all; but they are deeply attached to their hunting dogs. Once, on an autumn walk, I found two lost beagles belonging to a neighbour and the occasion of their return was celebrated with much pastis.

One Scotsman did not just pooh-pooh French hunting; everything French was an abomination to him, apart from the monuments which were mercifully dead. Doctor Tobias Smollett, that acerbic surgeon, had the prejudices of Nancy Mitford's Uncle Matthew in *The Pursuit of Love* – 'Wogs begin at Calais' and 'Abroad is unutterably bloody and all foreigners fiends'. He typifies the smug insularity of the British Grand Tourist.

Smollett was in the avant-garde, visiting Provence in November 1763. No one can say he and his ilk were not adventurous; by 1785, according to Gibbon, forty thousand Britons were loose in Europe; you could even cross the Alps by sedan chair.

Passing under the Pont-St-Esprit on a barge was enough to get Smollett going: 'It is not comparable to the bridge of Westminster, either for beauty or solidarity.'

As for two washerwomen, washing their children's 'clouts' in a Roman Bath, the Doctor was incensed: 'Surprised and disgusted at this filthy phenomenon, I asked by what means, and by whose permission, those dirty hags had got down to the basin, in order to contaminate the water at its fountainhead?'

The redeeming quality of Smollett is his sour humour. 'All the inns of this country are execrable,' he declares. But with a disarming display of *le fairplay Scottish* (perhaps because of the Mary Queen of Scots connection), he finds his fellow travellers' naïvety largely to blame. And the victims are *English*, naturally.

'The imposition is owing to the concourse of English

PONT-ST-ESPRIT, THE RHONE RIVER

ST-ANDRE-DE-ROQUEPERTUIS

the French who frequented her house, instead of using the seat, left their offerings on the floor, which she was obliged to have cleaned three or four times a day. This is a degree of beastliness which would appear detestable even in the capital of North Britain.'

Smollett's *Travels Through France and Italy* were attended by colic, vapours, spasms and bowel disorders; no wonder he saw Provence with a jaundiced eye. A more enthusiastic Scotsman, and more adventurous, was Robert Louis Stevenson whose *Travels With A Donkey* many consider to be his finest work.

Once again I take compiler's licence, and extend my borders west of Provence to the highlands of the Cévennes. These are clearly visible from our house on a mistless day, a constant reminder of Stevenson's precarious partnership with Modestine, that bitch of a donkey.

His trek, some hundred miles south from Le Monastier, near Le Puy, through the Massif Central to the Cévennes was typical of his vision of himself – writer as hero. Stevenson was a great self-dramatist. He knew about Jekyll and Hyde from his interior conflict – the Calvinist and the Bohemian, Victorian guilt and therapeutic exteriorisation, work as virtue and weapon against bourgeois society. From a much-travelled family – builders of lighthouses all over the world – Stevenson

who come hither, and, like simple birds of passage, allow themselves to be plucked by the people of the country who know their weak side, and make their attacks accordingly.'

Food had also to be fought for. 'As I was not disposed to eating stinking fish, with ragouts of eggs and onions, I insisted upon a leg of mutton, and a brace of fine partridges, which I found in the larder.'

I would not have liked the scavenging Doctor Smollett as a house guest, though he is sympathetic to a *patronne* who has just installed an indoor lavatory in her inn. 'All

ST-VICTOR–DE-MALCUP, R.L. STEVENSON COUNTRY

was the Scotsman for all places, adaptable traveller in California, France, and the South Seas. Because of ill health, each venture was a challenge of the will, of the mind over bodily infirmity. Unlike Smollett, there is no moaning and groaning about ailments, indeed not even a headache is mentioned in the whole tale.

Stevenson was too busy to be ill. 'I was looked upon with contempt, like a man who should project a journey to the moon…' First there was trouble with his luggage. 'The pad would not stay on Modestine's back for half a moment.' Then there was trouble with the donkey; a peasant taught him 'the masonic cry of the donkey-driver. "Proot!"…I prooted like a lion, I prooted melli-fluously like a sucking-dove; but Modestine would be neither softened nor intimidated.' Then there were im-aginary troubles – a very special wolf known as 'the beast', who 'ate women and children and shepherdesses celebrated for their beauty.'

Once on his way, Stevenson found travel traumas vanishing in the majesty of outdoor life. 'Night after night, in my own bedroom in the country, I have given ear to the perturbing concert of the wind among the woods…' It is not a mere lyrical acceptance – it is perturbing, with an awareness of something uncertain and unknown. A secret world. Later in the journey, he

becomes more sure of himself and it. 'The outer world, from which we cower into our houses seemed after all a gentle and habitable place, and night after night a man's bed, it seemed, was laid and waiting for him in the fields, where God keeps an open house.'

Gazing up from his bed at 'a faint silvery vapour', hearing 'the indescribable quiet talk of the runnel over the stones', Stevenson, like Giono, is master of evoking sensual pleasure. His only regret seems to be in sharing his idyll with no one but Modestine, hardly the most romantic of companions. 'And to live out of doors with

MOURRE NEGRE, ON TOP OF THE LUBERON

the woman a man loves is of all our lives the most complete and free.'

In these days of guarded camping sites, Stevenson's trek a hundred years ago, unarmed and alone, seems almost foolhardy. Indeed a merchant warned him: 'The English have always long purses, and it might very well enter into someone's head to deal you a blow some night.'

When I was twenty, I slept out at Sénas, on the banks of the Durance under a September night sky, with nothing to fear but mosquitoes. Then a terrible change came. It was the slaughter of the Drummond family, near Forcalquier in the fifties, that gave a dangerous name to casual camping.

Two peaceful families were destroyed in this crime by the Durance, where the land has a burnt-out look which constantly reminded Giono of ancient Greece and its tragedies. The two families were the Drummonds, middle-class British holidaymakers; and the Dominicis, Provençal peasants who owned the land where the Drummonds camped.

Dominici, respected old patriarch, after too many drinks with friends, went out into the night with a gun to do the rounds of his property. Did he, in his drunken state, mistake the Drummonds for marauders? Or was it premeditated murder? Or the crime of another? We shall never know. There was shaky proof and no witnesses; but the case was brilliantly brought against Dominici and he was condemned to life imprisonment (he was later released). It brought death to the Drummonds and lasting disgrace to the Dominicis.

Stevenson encountered a tragedy less dramatic, though a constant fear of winegrowers. Phylloxera. As his journey with Modestine brought him down into the wine-growing area of the Vivarais, he found it stricken at harvest time with vines ravaged by a kind of green-fly called phylloxera. '…I found a party of men working with a cider-press. I could not at first make out what they were after, and asked one fellow to explain. "Making cider," he said. "Oui, c'est ça. Comme dans le nord!" There was a ring of sarcasm in his voice; the country was going to the devil.'

Many of the young vines replacing those lost in the great phylloxera crisis came from California; so it is only fair that California should nowadays be making the French sit up and take notice of them as rivals – with their advanced technology and seduction of experts from Bordeaux.

BOLLENE, THE CANAL DE DONZERE

TULETTE

SIMIANE-LA-ROTONDE

As California progresses, so do the wines of the Midi which – apart from a few labels like Châteauneuf-du-Pape, Gigondas, Tavel – were until quite recently lumped together as Côtes-du-Rhône. To the south-west was something known as the wine lake, over-production and winegrowers protesting violently at foreign wines entering the Languedoc; to the south-east Bandol and Cassis, degenerating into nauseous plonk the nearer you got to Nice.

Midi wines were more sung about than having their praises sung. Brassens, remembering his youth at Sète, invents bacchanalian origins for himself in *Le Vin*.

My folk aren't at all
The kind you would call
Refeened.
I come from that ilk
Which October's milk
Has weaned.

That birthplace of mine
Was under a vine,
Thank God!
No cabbage or stork,
Before I could walk,
I trod!

Mistral is less intimate, more in his vigorous epic style, mixing Roman mythology with grass-roots folklore.

As bare as a brave gladiator,
Comes Bacchus, the great celebrator,
Leading the wine treaders' dance,
Off to the harvest of Crau.
The must of the grapes soon is staining
Their legs while the level is gaining,
And soon from the wine-press it's draining.
Into the depths of the vat,
The foaming new wine starts to flow.

(*Mireille*)

Rhythms, images, narrative (even when tragic) – Mistral seems to imbue everything with a relentless jollity.

For Giono there was something apocalyptic about the wine-harvest, because of wine's sacramental association with blood. In *Jean Le Bleu* a village at the end of the

RICHERENCHES, AFTER EVENING RAIN

harvest smells of dregs, the mud at the bottom of the vats, crushed stalks; strong men at the press struggle to squeeze the last drop from their grapes. With the drunken power of the gods, they seem to be crushing life out of what they have created. The metaphor is both Christian and pagan.

But wine is life-blood, too. Giono celebrates the therapeutic quality of wine among other natural cures. 'There were love herbs. There was the black flesh of hare caught in the best of hills. There was the strength of fire. There was dark wine.' (*Que Ma Joie Demeure*) Marcel Pagnol with equal respect gives us César's devotion to duty: 'I shall never leave my bar. I shall die mixing a kir, and if it were allowed, I'd have myself buried under the counter. What? You think I'm going to leave Marseille?' (*César*)

My own pleasure in wine is plebeian: visiting the small growers in the area, finding a new one, buying twenty litres, bottling it myself. If I'm very proud of a new discovery, I try it out on a singular wine buff. Minty Lalanne, who is Australian, gets my vote as the stranger most integrated into Provençal preserves; we go tasting together and she pronounces in hushed tones upon a Visan red or a Vinsobres rosé or a Laudun white as though some spy may be listening to her secret. With wine discoveries, we keep our mouths shut except when drinking.

Suspense runs through the wine-harvest with Hitchcockian intensity. Will the autumn rain hold off? Rain can cause fungus, delays, and costly keeping-on of the harvesters, students from all over – Montreal, Leeds, or Dakar – and even Marseille prostitutes.

When the autumn storms begin, we really know it. In *L'Ane Culotte*, Henri Bosco describes their approach: 'The earth soon begins to deliver to the heavens the reserves of electricity it has accumulated during the heat of summer. The air becomes heavy; even the stones of Les Belles-Tuiles enter into contact with the spirit of storms.' Southern rain usually arrives in a great cloudburst: Marseille has been known to surpass in one night the *annual* rainfall of Paris. Your roof had better be in good shape; ours isn't. We are constantly shifting tiles to cover up holes, putting off the evil hour of a proper roof job.

'The rain. The fountain sang in unison with it under the tree. Goudrun approached, back bent under the deluge. "Sod the rain. Every time I go to fetch my hay, it does this!"' (Giono: *Colline*) But after the deluge, the miraculous smell of its cleansing. 'The earth gave off a vague odour of mallow and wet clay.' (Bosco: *Le Mas Théotime*)

SEGURET

In November 1983 a tempest hit our house, in one of the worst storms of the century. These century record-breakers occur in Provence at least one autumn in five. Insurance companies send their experts who view the damage and the builder's estimate with deep suspicion: what was the roof like before the storm, they ask themselves? And slash the estimate in half. Visiting my Paris insurer, I asked him when I'd get paid. He looked sadly at the dossiers. 'Don't worry, M'sieur, you are in the pipeline.' I commiserated with him on the amount of claims he seemed to have this year. 'This *year*?' he exclaimed. 'M'sieur More, this pile is just the night of your tempest!'

Like the spring reflowering, rivers swollen with melting snow in spring now repeat the exercise with the autumn rains. Henry James, visiting Provence in 1884, arrived just in time for the floods. 'It has brought home to me that the *populations rurales* have many different ways of suffering, and my heart glowed with a grateful sense of cockneyism.' Cockneyism, in the American sense of being a town-dweller. In fact, James found much of Vaucluse too 'cockneyfied'. 'It is not only we in America, therefore, who besmirch our scenery; the practise exists in a more organized form (like everything else in France), in the country of good taste.'

We can all carry on about the utilities – vile electric pylons on our doorstep, hideous hypermarkets, squalid motels, and industrial zones. From our vantage point, it is too glib to curse the uglier aspects of modern society which, with typical schizophrenia, we all contribute to in one way or another. But, if one is a visitor not a wage-slave, they need not be in one's picture of Provence. Like me, James had no complaints about the walking. '...and as I went on it seemed that true happiness would consist in wandering through such a land on foot, on September afternoons, when one might stretch one's self on the

CAVAILLON, THE DURANCE RIVER

CERESTE

illuminates the vastness like an arc lamp, seeps into the sharp-edged cracks like a pin spot. 'Let us cry Long Live The Sun which gives us such a beautiful light,' wrote Cézanne to Emile Zola, in that very same November that Henry James was enjoying it.

It was one of Van Gogh's thousand reasons for coming south. 'Wishing also to see a different light, thinking that to look at nature under a brighter sky might give us a better idea of the Japanese way of feeling and drawing.' Cézanne was certain it was here, in the direct light of Provence not the reflected glory of the Louvre, that a young painter would learn his craft: '…you should get out there and live in yourself, in contact with nature, instincts, the sensation of art which inhabits us.'

Van Gogh had already found himself, capturing in his painting that Gionian roundness of the seasons, the movement of autumn into winter. '…and then the soil is covered, as with a carpet, by a thick layer of yellow and orange fallen leaves. And they are still falling like flakes of snow.'

warm ground in some shady hollow and listen to the hum of bees and the whistle of melancholy shepherds…'

Nor did the light ever cease to amaze him. 'It was a pleasure to be in Provence again – a land where the silver grey earth is impregnated with the light of the sky.'

After a storm the air is limpid and clear, the sun

ETANG DE GALABERT, SUNSET ON LAGOON

AURIBEAU, TOWARDS THE ALPS

CAVAILLON, DAWN ON THE DURANCE RIVER

·WINTER·

Snow fell our first Christmas Eve at Visan.

At a mere 300 metres above sea level as far south as Vaucluse, this is rare. And thrilling. It was a good augury. We had little more in the house than a bed, a primus stove, and a pair of tatty Art Deco armchairs; we were in that beautiful unclobbered state before a house becomes a home, that space, that pause, without the impedimenta and treasures of a lifetime and their associations.

The house, seen in its naked state, was full of friendly household ghosts. The walls with other people's picture hangers and empty corners cried out to be filled; and now that they have been, I have a nostalgia for the raw material of our first days. One white cat, as soft and clean as the snow, used to come pining for her lover, departed with the former owners; when the smell of cat left the kitchen, she came no more.

That snowfall of our first Christmas was nothing much, just a few centimetres in depth. But well before

VISAN

ST-MAURICE-SUR-EYGUES, VINEYARD IN SNOW

breakfast a snow-plough was clearing our track. The vine-stocks and cutback shoots in the vineyards around us made abstract patterns on the slopes, black dotted lines on pure white. Our neighbour Pierre had stripped one field of old vines after the harvest and this was totally white like a ski slope. At one edge were piles of old vine-stocks; Pierre said we could take what we wanted for firewood. It seemed weird to be brushing snow off wood associated with wine, and burning it on an open fire. The smoke has an exquisite nose; anyone who has barbecued with vine-shoots spurns lesser fuels.

Midi weather is at all times maverick. In mid-August a dinner for eighteen had to be hustled indoors from the terrace in the wake of a sudden cloudburst; last Christmas Day we had a brunch of smoked salmon, scrambled eggs and Bucks Fizz on that same terrace in warm sunshine. The Marquise de Sévigné would have been pleased; she seems to have had worse luck on her winter visits to her daughter at Grignan. On 3 February 1695 she wrote to her cousin Monsieur de Coulanges:

'Madame de Chaulnes writes me that I am too lucky to be here basking in sunshine: she believes that all our days are spun with gold and silk. Alas, dear cousin, we are a hundred times colder than Paris, exposed to every wind imaginable: either it's the south wind, or the north wind,

PONT-ST-ESPRIT, BRIDGE OVER THE RHONE

or the devil, or whatever wind will torment us, fighting among themselves to have the honour of shutting us in our rooms; all our rivers are plagued; even the angry Rhône cannot resist; our desks are glacial, our pens riveted to fingers numbed with cold; all we breathe is snow, our mountains are delightful in their excess of horror; I can't wait for an artist to express the full ghastliness of our beauty: that is where we are.'

I hate to disagree with such a witty letter writer, but winter is my favourite season: I expect less, I find more. Also there seems to be less odd-jobbing, grass and weeds

hibernate, and as long as nobody nicks our fuel for the heating and there is enough firewood, I have for once time to stop and look around me, read, play music, and truly have the pleasure of the place. 'Lucky Midi,' wrote Colette. 'It has, from January, daffodils, almonds, mimosa in great yellow clouds, pinks, anemones, while the rest of France is still stiff with cold.' (*Belles Saisons I*)

The nineteenth century American writer, Nathaniel Hawthorne, shares my love of winter twilight.
'…after the sunset, the horizon burned and glowed with a rich crimson and orange lustre, looking at once warm and cold. After it grew dark, the stars brightened, and Miss M – from her window pointed out some of the planets to the children, she being as familiar with them as a gardener with his flowers. They were bright as diamonds.'

Provence in winter reminded him of New England before the snow has fallen – bleak, barren, and bare.

Alphonse Daudet finds enchantment in the salt-water lagoon of Vaccarès, its flora and fauna in winter twilight making up for the boring nothingness of the Camargue coastline. The birds fishing on the banks: duck, heron, bittern, flamingo and 'the real ibis from Egypt'. And the horses – 'In fact, from where I sit, not a sound can I hear but a lapping of water and the *gardien*'s voice rounding

ETANG DE VACCARES, TWILIGHT

heavy truck floundering with one wheel in the water, a bridge collapsed beneath it, its driver cursing the Commune for not strengthening the shore roads against the violence of the waves.

But these dikes in winter are the preserve of sunset hunters – poised with their tripods and telefoto lenses. Wildlife, picture postcards, or that extraordinary moment when sky and water become one, whatever their game, there is a tranquil expectancy.

> Swans and flamingoes are flying,
> Scoters and heron are crying,
> They come when the daylight is dying,
> To perch on the banks of the ponds,
> And hail the last rays of the sun.
>
> (Mistral: *Mireille*)

up his horses ranging round the banks. They all have resonant names: Cifer! …(Lucifer)…L'Estello! …L'Esternello! Each horse, hearing his name, trots up, mane flying in the wind, coming to eat oats from the *gardien's* hand.'

Driving out on the Vaccarès dikes is strictly forbidden in rough weather. Waves can sweep your car into the waters of the wild-life sanctuary; Carey and I found a

Giono in his vision of the roundness of things, saw the sun dying when it set. The sun is associated with the time of labour which is probably hard and painful and not for pleasure; the sun is the enemy. We strangers from the north fleeing our long dark days, find this hard to understand, especially in winter when there is no danger of

COUSTELLET, MORNING MIST

sunstroke. But it is there, all the year round, omnipresent; in its day it brings both fruit and torment; at night we are safe from it, either way.

'The sun, dead, emptied itself like an egg below the earth, and night fell. Then – but only if we are wise – we walk calmly towards the fountains in the dark shadows of the night.' (*Rondeur des Jours*)

. The sun, as enemy, bleaches the high plateau white in summer, then disappears and lets in the white frost in winter; white is the colour of death, the face of a sick man is white. White not black has the diabolic connotation in Giono's occult.

Days in December centre round the lead-up to Les Fêtes – the quiet family Noël and the wild dance-till-dawn of St-Sylvèstre or New Year's Eve. While out-of-work actors jingle their bells outside Printemps, Macy's and Selfridges, here Les Hippys (as they are still affectionately called) come down from their mountain farms and potteries to sell home-grown turkeys and home-thrown pots. Business is brisk in the markets of Provence despite the wind howling through the stalls like a banshee, where only the ubiquitous pizza-pedlars keep warm over the travelling ovens in their vans.

This is Giono's 'land of the wind', the pre-Christmas mighty rushing. Hurricane force gales hit the flat, unpro-tected Camargue: '*vira la bano au gisele*' is Provençal for turning horns to the wind. Bulls' necks are strong, take the force of it, the weaker animals are protected by their massive hulks behind which they cower in fear. 'And God help a herd that does not obey this law.' Alphonse Daudet tells of panicked herds running, blinded by the rain, headlong into the raging waters of the Vaccarès like Gadarene swine.

In Henri Bosco's *L'Ane Culotte* there is a feeling of anticipation, not menace, at the coming of winter. 'Through the little School's north-facing windows they

MONTEILS

CAMARET, CHRISTMAS WITH TRAVELLING PIZZA

MIRABEL-AUX-BARONNIES

could see the first snow passing over the crests. Already stoves had been lit and the classes smelt of damp wool and leather. Probably by now, on the heights, wild animals looking for warmer pastures had shifted their habitat. All the chimneys were smoking over the village, and with a great noise carts emptied vine-shoots outside the baker's.'

Children and animals: the Provençal Christmas is one of the world's most Christmasy. I confess to a Scrooge-like antipathy to city merriment, office-party retching, and porky bleariness as one hiccups and dozes through *The Sound of Music* on telly for the umpteenth time. But the spirit of Christmas south is a very different matter; it is strictly a family affair.

The Day is not as important as the Eve – the night of the Crèches Provençales. The most popular of these is the Crèche Vivante – a nativity play before Midnight Mass, with a live lamb which bleats sleepily through the sermon. It is acted by local children from infants to teenagers, with good-humoured, slightly pissed priests keeping the younger ones awake with prods and hisses.

A Crèche Vivante is the hottest ticket in town, and you have to book for Les Baux or Séguret months in advance. In the smaller villages – Sainte-Cécile-des-Vignes or Mirabel-aux-Baronnies, it is safe to arrive an hour before for a good seat. Thermal underwear *de rigueur*.

By including local folklore, the Nativity takes on an immediacy beyond mere ritual. Pagan goddesses seem to have been invited too: buxom, black-eyed girls in Provençal costume – surely one of the prettiest with its black velvet waistcoat laced up over frothy white blouse and voluminous print skirts over white petticoats. They brandish garlands of vineleaves and sheaves of corn as they dance up and down the aisles, to the music of fife and drum and the flash of Minoltas from proud parents.

After or before the Midnight Mass, there is the Reveillon dinner, described by Lawrence Durrell in

TULETTE, CHRISTMAS EVE

Monsieur. The scene is the Château of Verfeuille, owned by Piers de Nogaret, who can no longer afford its upkeep and sadly fears this may be the last Christmas with his friends and retainers, its traditional ceremonies all the more poignant and to be carried out correctly. The oldest and youngest members of the household go out and choose the Yule Log.

'It was paraded thrice around the long supper table and then laid down before the great hearth, while old Jan undertook to preside over the ceremony of the libation which he did with great polish, filling first of all a tall jar of *vin cuit*.'

The Yule Log is blessed in Provençal.

'And as he reached the last words of the incantation which were "Christmas has arrived" a huge bundle of vine-trimmings was set alight under the Ceremonial log and the whole fireplace flamed up, irradiating the merry faces of the company, as if they had caught fire from sympathy with the words, and now everyone embraced anew and clapped hands, while the old man once more filled the ceremonial bowl with wine, but this time passed it about as a loving-cup, beginning with little Tounin the youngest child; and so on in order of seniority until at last it came back to his hand.'

We of the northern blow-out imagine the French to make equal pigs of themselves at the Reveillon dinner. This is not so in Provence.

'By an old tradition it has always been a "lean" supper, so that in comparison with other feast days it might have seemed a trifle frugal. Nevertheless the large dish of *raito* exhaled a wonderful fragrance; this was a ragout of mixed fish in a sauce flavoured with wine and capers.'

Durrell's continuing menu includes chicken flamed with cognac, Rhône pan-fish, white cod, snails and *cardons* (giant thistle stems in white sauce). 'The flavour is one of the most exquisite one can encounter in the southern regions of France; yet it is only a common field vegetable.' The light repast ends with 'sweetmeats and nuts and winter melons'.

In contrast to Durrell's exuberance and relish, Ezra Pound, 'wining the ghosts of yester-year,' seems to experience, far away from home at a poignant time, that yearning of the stranger for familiar shades.

'I am homesick after mine own kind,
Oh I know that there are folk about me, friendly faces,
But I am homesick after mine own kind.'

(*In Durance*, 1907)

PONT-ST-ESPRIT, A VIEW FROM THE BRIDGE

Colette, however, loved to indulge her sweet tooth at this time.

'The inn's table groans with marzipan cakes, crystalized fruits, Provençal sweetmeats sugared and sugared again; a bah-ahing outside tells us Midnight Mass has just finished and that the shepherds are bringing their lambs back, blessed beneath their capes.' (*Belles Saisons I*)

The second Fête is more epicurean than Christmas – the St-Sylvèstre feast on New Year's Eve. Country inns charge £40 a head for a six-course meal and Rabalaisian roistering, and it has become the custom to avoid these fancy prices by friends clubbing together and feasting at home. Farmers push the boat out with Dom Perignon and Chivas Regal, and a gargantuan dinner. It can be a male chauvinist nightmare, however, for whoever gets to be hostess: a woman friend described the men eating two trout and three dozen oysters each while their ladies sweated over the roasting of two geese on a spit. When the geese were ready, the men looked surprised. 'What's *that*?' they asked, already sated with food; and left the geese to the women who were by then too hot and tired to eat.

On January the First begins the long hangover. Hibernation. Digging in and forgetting the outside world. 'We have decided,' wrote the Marquis de Sade in his usual blunt manner from Lacoste in 1774, 'for a thousand reasons to see very little of the world this winter. As a result I pass the evening in my study, and Madame and her women busy themselves in a neighbouring room till bedtime, which means, at nightfall, the castle is irreversibly shut, lights out, no one cooking, and often no provisions. Consequently I beg of you not to put us out by arriving for dinner, and don't put us out in any event.'

No amateur theatricals, even. The Marquis used to put on plays at his theatre in the château, preparing himself

GORGES DE LA CEZE

for his later role as impressario-director of the lunatics at the Charenton asylum where he was to become an inmate. This primitive therapy was the subject of the play *Marat-Sade*.

What, one wonders, was he doing in his study all alone on those winter's nights? Penning his pornography? Writing disagreeable letters to friends? Or to future Revolutionaries with whom he was to side in the hopes of preserving his aristocratic privileges in the new Republic when it came? More likely he was preparing yet another defence against his accusers, the self-righteous bourgeois notables and the justices of the Parlement d'Aix: '...seven or eight powdered mopheads, to whom I owe my trouble, one just back from sleeping with a girl he's debauched, the other with the wife of his best friend, another escaping shamefully down a blind alley where he would be furious to have it known what he just did there...'

Others spend even quieter evenings. 'It's freezing hard, we have a good fire and, despite a certain edginess, our minds are clear and our souls in good shape,' writes Henri Bosco, describing country people, restless at being cooped up in the depths of winter. They have a longing for travel, yet a horror of travelling. 'Feet up by the fire, in a half sleep that is so conducive to the marvels procured for us by sluggish warmth and the dancing of magic figures in the embers, we create the men and countries we need to disturb us pleasurably – without taking one step.' (*Sylvius*)

Another pleasurable indoor activity Bosco describes in *Le Mas Théotime*: the drying of herbs and classifying them in a fire-warmed attic. 'I could see them and breathe their delicate smell; and I'd say their names just for myself, just for me who had collected them during the summer. I spoke them at the top of my voice without fear of being heard. For I had no other happiness than to live, hidden from the world, in this attic, among the plants and flowers of the fields.'

AIX-EN-PROVENCE, ST-SAUVEUR CATHEDRAL

PONT-ST-ESPRIT, QUAYSIDE

SEGURET

If the weather is wet, outdoor pipe-smoking has a special joy, according to Giono. '…the pipe takes on another taste: the taste of alleys and tracks, the taste of dead leaves, of leaf-mould and the natural fertilizers of the forest's great roots.' (*Que Ma Joie Demeure*)

A minimum of activity goes on outdoors. Lone figures in balaclavas, dark glasses, anoraked like eskimos work in the stripped vineyards. I walked one day beneath an ice-blue sky, a mistral piercing clothing and body to the bone. Coming and going on the wind, now loud, now soft, now not at all, there was the most beautiful sound of keening Arabic quarter-tones: on the crest of a hill a solitary Algerian vineyard worker was singing a plaintive song I imagined to express longing for his homeland and loved ones across the sea.

It is a season of solitude. Villages seem deserted; if it were not for the smoke of the chimneys, it would appear no one lived in them. The Algerian sits, expressionless, in the café, waiting. Waiting for spring.

Alone at the asylum in St-Rémy Van Gogh continued to work. He wrote to Theo on 3 February 1889: 'I must tell you this, that the neighbours, etc., are particularly kind to me; as everyone suffers here either from fever or hallucinations, or madness, we understand each other like members of the same family.' The following winter, his courage never deserting him, he wrote: 'I hope to get myself used to working in the cold – in the morning there are very interesting effects of white frosts and fog, then I still have a great desire to do for the mountains and the cypresses what I have just done for the olives, and have a good go at them.'

A deathliness seems to have taken hold of the land and villages in their deserted wintry state. But it is not morbid. In the roundness of the seasons, everything has its place – even death. 'Like all men of the sun, the old man let himself be seduced by the temptation of the cold. Clearly he preferred death to life, and, after much coughing (with a cough strangely reminiscent of the melancholy sound of cattle lost in the night) he remained stiff and soundless on his camp bed.' (Giono: *Ennémonde*)

PONT-ST-ESPRIT, CEMETERY

ST-PANTALEON-LES-VIGNES, VINEYARD WITH WINE AD

·THE DAYS ARE ROUND·

An old man waits for death, the end of his winter. And in the same book, Giono has an old lady wait for spring.

'It will come, no doubt about it, some day or other, soon. She is on her day-bed. Amorphous as a mixture of flour and water and salt, with a fresh doughiness which still has to be kneaded a bit this evening, but which tomorrow will be worked on with a rolling-pin to give it a useful shape. Yes, the spring will come.' (*Ennémonde*)

Where the frosts have hardened the ground, on the snowy highlands, the thaw begins – with a great collapse of the sky.

'It is the rain cloud, the wind from the four corners, the loud song of trees with dry leaves, obstinate oaks which have kept their foliage from the past year and speak in the wind with a torrent's voice.' (Giono: *Regain*)

All round us this strange, long-lasting gold of the oak trees suddenly begins to depart as the new buds push the old leaves off. Nature comes back into action, first a little

COMPS, GOATS PICNIC

creakily, then in leaps and bounds – almond blossom in February, daffodils in March, the vines' first tendrils in April. 'I knew nothing of a spring which proceeds by explosions,' Colette wrote to a friend in April 1928. 'How suddenly the roses bloom! Here I shall ripen.'

Smelling the gentian that the March mistral blows off the hills, Monsieur Seguin's goat is eager to be off from that boring farm and up there with the sheep in the fresh spring air and to hell with the wolves.

And Rudyard Kipling, motoring through Provence in 1933, when not nearly killing jay-walking peasants and being killed himself by humped-back bridges, is an unexpected witness to the miracle of spring's return.

'For those who love the land and its people, March is the month above all; for then France, who never stops working, begins her spring cleaning, loppings, and prunings … The roads are made interesting by the dung-carts, the huge bundles of new vine-stocks, and the freshly-ordered, brightly painted agricultural implements … The strength of France is in her soil. If you stood one hundred Frenchmen on their heads, you would find the plough-mould on the boots of at least seventy-five … They give *La Terre* the reverence they deny other gods; and she repays their worship.' (*Souvenirs of France*)

Now Carey and I have come full circle. The roundness of our year is nearly complete. We have tried to convey our gut reaction to Provence, our response to its atmosphere, its emanations. A feeling that made us come and makes us glad we stayed.

'And though we have saved nothing, we have danced the *carmagnole*; and, except for the day when my wife took the mosquito lotion for a mouth wash, and the time when I tried to smoke a French cigarette, and, as Ring Lardner would say, swooned, we haven't been sorry we came.' (F. Scott Fitzgerald: *How to Live on Practically Nothing a Year*)

Provence could take Scott and Zelda, as it has taken all kinds of strangers in its stride, including us. It is a mongrel, a mixture of races related not by nationality but by nature – the roundness of days, seasons, all things which unite and absorb us all. From Giono, the last words: 'There is no Provence. Whoever loves it, loves the world.'

CAIRANNE

A C K N O W L E D G M E N T S

Thanks for permission to reprint are due to:–

BERNARD GRASSET:
From *Regain* by Jean Giono © Bernard Grasset 1930, *Que Ma Joie Demeure* by Jean Giono © Bernard Grasset 1935, *Colline* by Jean Giono © Bernard Grasset 1929.

GALLIMARD:
From *Rondeur des Jours (L'Eau Vive I)* by Jean Giono © Gallimard 1943, *Le Jardin d'Hyacinthe* by Henri Bosco © Gallimard 1946, *Le Mas Théotime* by Henri Bosco © Gallimard 1952, *Sylvius* by Henri Bosco © Gallimard 1970.

PETER OWEN LTD:
From *Ennémonde* by Jean Giono © Gallimard 1968.

OXFORD UNIVERSITY PRESS:
From *L'Ane Culotte* by Henri Bosco, published in English as *Culotte The Donkey* trans. Sister Mary Theresa McCarthy © Oxford University Press 1978.

THE MARCEL PAGNOL ESTATE:
From *Marius* © Fasquelle 1928, *César* © Fasquelle 1946, *La Gloire de Mon Père* published in English as *The Days Were Too Short* by Hamish Hamilton (UK) and Doubleday (US) © Marcel Pagnol 1976. All titles by Marcel Pagnol.

THE COLETTE ESTATE:
From *Belles Saisons I* © Flammarion 1955, *Paysages et Portraits* © Flammarion 1958, *Prisons et Paradis* © Ferenczi 1932, *Bella-Vista* © Ferenczi 1937. All titles by Colette.

EDITIONS MUSICALES 57:
From *La Ballade des Gens Qui Sont Nés Quelque Part* by Georges Brassens © Editions Musicales 57 1972, *Le Vin* by Georges Brassens © Editions Musicales 57 1957, *Dans l'Eau de la Claire Fontaine* by Georges Brassens © Editions Musicales 57 1962.

AD PETERS & CO LTD:
From *The Pursuit of Love* by Nancy Mitford, published by Hamish Hamilton © Nancy Mitford 1945, *The Blessing* by Nancy Mitford, published by Hamish Hamilton © Nancy Mitford 1951. Permission granted on behalf of the Nancy Mitford Estate.

DEBORAH ROGERS LTD:
From *The Unquiet Grave* by Cyril Connolly, published by Hamish Hamilton © Cyril Connolly 1944. Permission granted on behalf of the Cyril Connolly Estate.

THE BODLEY HEAD:
From *Tender Is The Night* by F. Scott Fitzgerald © Charles Scribner's Sons 1933 Renewal © 1961 © Charles Scribner's Sons 1934 Renewal © Frances S.F. Lanahan 1962, *How to Live on Practically Nothing a Year* by F. Scott Fitzgerald © Saturday Evening Post 1924.

FABER & FABER:
From *Collected Shorter Poems* by Ezra Pound (*Sestina: Altaforte, Villonaud For This Yule, In Durance*) © Ezra Pound 1926. From *Livia* by Lawrence Durrell © Lawrence Durrell 1978, *Monsieur* by Lawrence Durrell © Lawrence Durrell 1974.

CURTIS BROWN LTD:
From *The Plant-Magic Man* by Lawrence Durrell © Lawrence Durrell 1973. Permission granted on behalf of Lawrence Durrell.

AP WATT LTD:
From *Souvenirs of France* by Rudyard Kipling © 1933 by Rudyard Kipling. Permission granted on behalf of The National Trust For Places of Historic Interest or Natural Beauty and Macmillan London Ltd.